Beginning Reading Instruction

Level 1A

B
Piper
Books

Instructions

Reader
- Say the sounds and read the word.
- When you know the word, just say it; there is no further need to say the sounds.
- No guessing! None! Read through the word.

Instructor
- Point out any letter/sound correspondences introduced in the new story.
- When the reader struggles with a word, tell them the correct sound(s) only after they have tried hard to remember.
- **Don't** try to provide any other help or explanation.
- Praise frequently, and end each session well before the reader becomes tired.

Story Discussion
- On completion of each story, if using the Questions encourage the learner to answer in full sentences and to reread the relevant page(s) if necessary.
- Many children will benefit from this increased scrutiny; others may benefit more from rereading or moving on to the next book.

See › www.piperbooks.co.uk › RESOURCES › BRI free resources for BRI Level 1 Initial and Mastery Assessments and a book-by-book Pupil Progress Sheet, including a record of word, sound and letter(s) introduction and a tutor comments column.

Contents

Story 1: **I See Sam**.................5

Story 2: **Sam**....................21

Story 3: **See Sam**.................37

Story 4: **See Me** 53

Story 5: **Mat** 69

Story 6: **See Mat**.................85

STORY 1

I See Sam

Story Synopsis

In his encyclopedia, Mat the Rat discovers a picture of a lion and learns many things about the big cats – what they look like, where they live, and what they eat. Excited by the drawings of what he assumes to be his friend Sam the Lion, Mat drags Sam over to the book and delights him with the pictures.

New Words	New Letter(s)/Sounds
I	'I' /ie/*
see	's' /s/
	'ee' /ee/
Sam	'a' /a/
	'm' /m/

The sound /ie/ has many spelling alternatives. Here the spelling is 'I'.

Speech, Language and Communication

Factual Questions

p7   What is Mat the Rat carrying?

p19   Who do Mat and Sam see in the book?

Developing Comprehension

p16   How do you think that Sam feels?

p19   Do Sam and Mat look happy or sad?

See.

See?

"I see. I see."

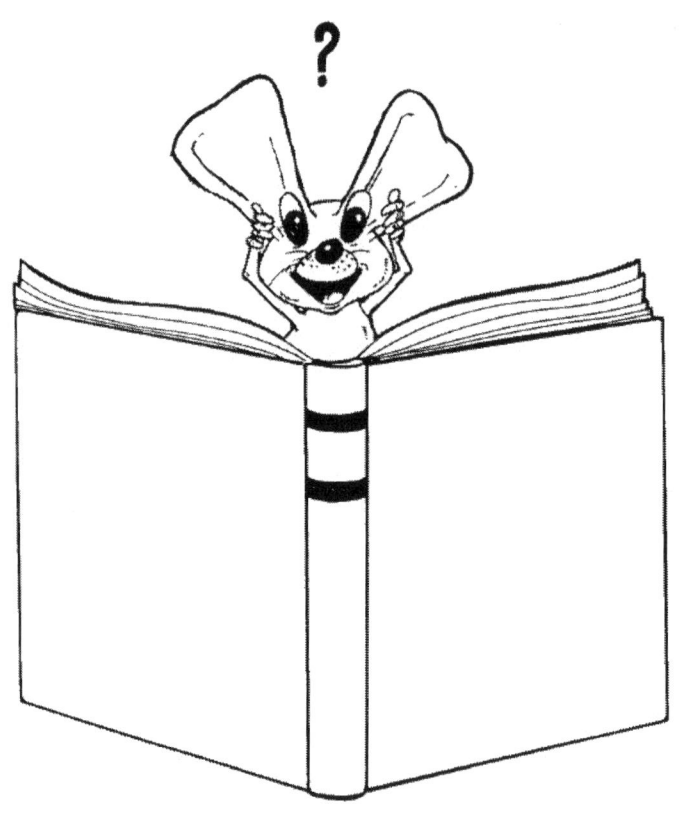

"Sam?"

"I see Sam."

"I see."

"Sam! Sam!"

"Sam! Sam! See Sam!"

"See Sam?"

"I see.
I see Sam!"

"See Sam!"

"I see Sam! I see Sam!"

Sam.

STORY 2

Sam

Story Synopsis

Mat the Rat gives Sam the Lion a cape and a crown. When Sam wears them he thinks he can do anything he wants. He sees a calf and decides to play "bullfighter". It is Sam, however, not the calf, who gets caught in the cape. Mat helps untangle Sam, and Sam is once more the smiling king of the jungle.

New Words   **New Letter(s)/Sounds**

(none)   (none)

Speech, Language and Communication

Factual Questions

p23 Can you remember what is in Mat the Rat's sack?

p33 How is Mat trying to help Sam?

Developing Comprehension

p29 Why is Mat running away?

p32 Where is Sam – *under* the cloak, *behind* the cloak, or *on top of* the cloak?

"I."

"I."

"Sam."

"See!"

"See Sam."

"I see."

See Sam.

See!

"Sam! Sam!"

"I see Sam."

See.

"I see Sam."

Sam!

Story 3

See Sam

Story Synopsis

Sam the Lion is strolling along engrossed in his book, not noticing the huge hole in front of his feet or Mat the Rat's attempts to warn him. Sam disappears. Mat is not sure what has happened and yells for Sam. Sam yells back from the bottom of the hole. Finally Mat finds a shovel and rescues his friend.

New Words   **New Letter(s)/Sounds**

am   (none)

Speech, Language and Communication

Factual Questions

p41 Why doesn't Sam see the hole?

p42 What happens to Sam?

Developing Comprehension

p42-43 How does Mat the Rat feel?

p50 How does Mat help Sam?

Sam

"I see Sam."

"Sam! Sam!"

"See!"

"Sam. Sam."

"See. See."

"I am Sam! I am Sam!"

"Sam? Sam?"

"I am Sam. See!"

"Sam! I see. I see."

"See!"

"See, Sam. See!"

"I see Sam. See! See!"

Sam.

STORY 4

See Me

Story Synopsis

Mat the Rat keeps shouting at Sam the Lion to look at him, but all Sam wants to do is sleep. Mat finally wakes Sam up by beating a big drum. Sam is furious and a chase ensues.

New Words	New Letter(s)/Sounds
me	'e' /ee/*

The sound /ee/ has many spelling alternatives. Here the spelling is 'e'.

Speech, Language and Communication

Factual Questions

p58-59 What is Sam doing?

p66 How does Mat the Rat wake Sam up?

Developing Comprehension

p59 Do you think that Mat looks *happy* or *puzzled* or *grumpy*?

Can you find pictures of Mat: Shouting – Running – Jumping – Banging a drum?

"Sam!"

"Sam! Sam!"

"I am Sam.
I am."

"Sam! See me."

See Sam.

"Sam, see me."

"See me."

"See me. See me."

"I see."

See.

"See me."

"Sam, see me!"

"I am Sam.
I am.
See me!"

"Sam!"

Story 5

Mat

Story Synopsis

Mat the Rat urges Sam the Lion to watch him paint. Sam naturally assumes that Mat is painting *him* and is none too pleased at the sight of Mat's self-portrait. Grabbing the brush, Sam cruelly adds a cage to the picture…whereupon Mat hurls the tin of paint at him.

New Words

Mat

New Letter(s)/Sounds

't' /t/

Speech, Language and Communication

Factual Questions

p77 What has Mat painted?

p84 Is that a hat on top of Sam's head?

Developing Comprehension

p77-78 Why is Sam cross with Mat?

p82 Why is Mat cross with Sam?

"I am Mat.
See me."

"I see Sam."

"See me, Sam."

See Mat.
See Sam.

"I see Mat."

Mat?

"See me.
See me, Sam!"

"I am Sam.
See me!"

"I see!"

See Mat.
See Sam.

"I see Mat.

See, Mat."

See Mat.

See Mat.

See Sam.

STORY 6

See Mat

Story Synopsis

The animals are playing school. Mat the Rat is trying to teach Sam the Lion, Mit the Chimp, and Sis the Snake how to read their names. He starts by writing 'S I S' in the sand. His pupils have some difficulty reading the name, and Mat finally has to 'say the sounds'. Sis is delighted and reads her name for her friends. Mat then writes the other names, including his own, and the animals all have fun reading.

New Words	New Letter(s)/Sounds
Sis	'i' /i/
Mit	(none)

Speech, Language and Communication

Factual Questions

p91 Who are Mat's pupils?

p92 Whose name does Mat first write in the sand?

Developing Comprehension

p87 Why is Mat standing behind a desk?

p99 Why is everyone looking so pleased?

"I am Mat. I see Sis."

"See me. I am Sis."

"I am Sam. See Mit."

"I am Mit."

See Mat. See Sam.
See Sis. See Mit.

"Sam! Sam!
I see Sam."

"I am Mit. Me, me!"

"Mit! Mit!
I see Mit."

"See S-i-s, Sis!

See Sis!"

"Sis. I am Sis! See me."

See Sis.

"See M-i-t, Mit.
See S-a-m, Sam."

See Sis. See Sam.
See Mit. See Mat.

Sis   Sam
Mit
Mat

Stories in
BRI: Beginning Reading Instruction Programme:

BRI Level 1A – 6 Stories
BRI Level 1B – 6 Stories
BRI Level 1C – 6 Stories
BRI Level 1D – 6 Stories

BRI Level 2A – 6 Stories
BRI Level 2B – 6 Stories
BRI Level 2C – 6 Stories
BRI Level 2D – 6 Stories

BRI Booster Book 1A – 5 Stories
BRI Booster Book 1B – 5 Stories
BRI Booster Book 1C – 5 Stories
BRI Booster Book 1D – 5 Stories

BRI Level 3A – 5 Stories
BRI Level 3B – 5 Stories
BRI Level 3C – 5 Stories
BRI Level 3D – 5 Stories

This edition of BRI (Beginning Reading Instruction) Level 1A
Published in 2020 by Piper Books Ltd
United Kingdom

www.piperbooks.co.uk
enquiries@piperbooks.co.uk

This updated book was designed, formatted and produced by Piper Books Ltd

Questions and synopses © Piper Books Ltd

Printed in Great Britain
by Amazon